ESTHER

ARE YOU READY FOR THE JOURNEY

FULFILLING GOD'S PURPOSE IN YOUR LIFE

Unless otherwise stated, all scripture is cited from the New King James Version of Bible at **www.biblegateway.com**

Book Coach – Robin Devonish
Cover Design – Okomota
Editing and Layout – Pen Publish Profit, LLC
Interior Design – Istvan Szabo, Ifj.

ISBN 13: 978-1-7370917-1-4

Printed in the United States of America

All the glory and praise for this book belong to God. **I dedicate this book to...**

My 93-year-old mom, a woman of great faith, prayer and who is obedient to God. She is still on her journey, fulfilling God's purpose for her life.

My Pastor W. Mosley, a man of prayer, great faith, and integrity. My Aunt Florine Mosley took me into her home at a crucial time in my life. She loved and cared for me until I could get back on my feet.

In Loving Memory...

I honor my late Leader and Founder, Helen McClung, who I lovingly called "Auntie." She started me on my journal and led me to the Lord.

I honor my Assistant Pastor, Edward McClung, my spiritual father, who supported me at critical times in my life.

I honor my dad, whose spiritual journey began in his senior years. God saved him, and he was an inspiration to me and many others.

I honor Nana and Papa Nisbett, my spiritual parents who provided love, spiritual guidance, and encouragement during my journey.

To all of my brothers, sisters, family, and friends who are part of my life, I love and appreciate you all.

I acknowledge...

Those who helped with my manuscript.

Thanks to my beloved husband and best friend, Marvin, for his encouragement, support, and valuable feedback when writing my manuscript.

Special thanks to my amazing sister Ruth (Rudy) Stephens and my wonderful brother-in-law Eric Stephens for repeatedly reading my manuscript from start to finish. Thanks for checking the grammar, spelling errors, and giving pointers. Thank you for always praying and supporting me.

Thanks to my incredible Big Sister Deborah Mosley. You have been a wonderful sister and mentor. Thank you for reading my manuscript, giving me feedback, and the many calls to find out how the book was progressing. Thanks for your support and prayers.

Thanks to my beautiful daughter Katie for your tireless efforts to read the manuscript and type the revisions. Thanks for helping to edit and providing constructive feedback, and taking time to help, although juggling work and school.

Thanks to my wonderful son Michael for his support and helping out, although he has a lot going on in his life, going to school and being an essential worker during this pandemic.

Thanks to Publisher Robin Devonish for turning my manuscript into a beautiful book that I pray will bless many readers.

FOREWORD

I am extremely grateful to Esther Luckett for the honor she has given me to write the forward for this book. Her book has caused me to stop and become more mindful of the journey that I am on. I have had the opportunity and privilege to have Esther engaged in various parts of my life journey, which is why I feel truly fortunate to write this foreword.

Esther has been a blessing to me as she has helped and supported me throughout my endeavors. I have earned two college degrees, completing a post-graduate advanced degree, a songwriter, and a Minister of the Gospel of Christ. Not only has she been a blessing to me throughout my journey, but she has also helped and assisted others in finding God's purpose for their life.

I am convinced that Esther was called to write this book because she lives her life's journey to God's glory. As a Sunday school teacher, Minister of the gospel, and church programs coordinator, she prayerfully goes about her God-given tasks. She is a fierce and tireless advocate for helping others find their purpose and building up the Kingdom of God. She is an inspiration to all who come in contact with her.

We are all on this journey called 'life,' and there are questions you may have asked yourself that this book will help you answer. We are all on a journey, but are we fulfilling God's purpose for our lives? As a traveler on the journey of life, do you know God's purpose for your life? Where we will end this journey depends on the choices we make. This book is a tool that will encourage and help you during your journey.

As a Professor, I am an avid reader of books. As a minister of the Gospel of Christ, I have read many devotional and spiritual books. I have had the opportunity to read this book more than once, and I have been blessed with new insights every time I have read it. In this must-read book, Esther Luckett gives us a view of various people who have and those who have not chosen to fulfill God's purpose for their life. You will meet people who sacrificed everything or went places that they had not gone before to fulfill God's purpose and the amazing results of their choice. This is a book that you should read. It will encourage and help you on your spiritual journey.

We all started our journey here on earth. As Christians, we will end our journey in glory with our Lord and Savior, Jesus Christ. What an incredible journey this is! It has ups and downs along the way, but we have a Savior who is walking along beside us, going before us, surrounding and protecting us as we travel along life's path. This book gives insights into how to travel life's journey and fulfill God's purpose for your life. Included are helpful tips and 'Rest Stops' that will cause you to stop and ponder the tasks, jobs, or responsibilities you have in your life. Once you read this book and take it to heart, it will profoundly impact your life.

If you have not started to fulfill God's purpose for your life, I encourage you to turn these pages and find out how you can! Congratulations on taking your first steps towards finding God's purpose for your life.
Are you ready to take this journey and fulfill God's purpose for your life? The journey of walking with the Lord is a journey you do not want to miss. Read this book!

Ruth Stephens, ABD
Founder of A-Zetta Business Services
Adjunct Professor, City University of New York

PREFACE

When people take a trip or travel to a specific destination, they choose the travel method best for them. Some people travel by plane, boat, bus, train, car, etc. The company providing the services usually has a slogan to catch the prospective travelers' attention.

I believe many may have heard this slogan, which has been around since 1956. "Go Greyhound and Leave the Driving to Us." This slogan was posted on Greyhound buses, seen on television, billboards, and in magazine advertisements. You could hear it on radio commercials promoting this way of travel. People appreciate taking a trip or journey without worrying about driving themselves. People who take Greyhound can relax, stretch their legs and rest until they have reached their destination. Greyhound provides listings of destinations, amenities, and benefits for the traveler.

While writing this book, the world was/is amid a Coronavirus pandemic. There is a ban on traveling. The airline industry has been impacted largely. People are restricted from traveling in some states, countries, and continents. However, there is one journey that a worldwide pandemic cannot stop. That is your journey with God in fulfilling your divine purpose and destiny.

Allow this book to take you on a spiritual journey to finding and fulfilling "God's divine purpose" for your life. By reading this book, you can travel to places you may have never been and meet people you have never met. These people chose to answer God's call for their lives and prospered by being obedient and having faith in God. These chosen people did great exploits with God's help.

Life is a journey. From the time God brings us into this world until the day we die, we are all on a journey. The choices you make determine where you will spend eternity. God has your past, present, and future in His hands. Accepting His call for your life is your choice to accept or reject. If you've decided to take the journey with the Lord, He promises to be with you always.

The good thing about this journey is that others have taken the journey before. They left a road map with a book of instruction inspired by Almighty God, Himself. The Bible contains guidance, information, and instructions to help you to fulfill your purpose. It is full of valuable information that will make your journey successful. You do not have to take this journey alone. God gives you a companion, comforter, the Holy Spirit to travel with you. God will direct you to the places you need to go and people you need to meet as you fulfill your commission to "go into the world and preach the gospel." He will get you safely from earth to heaven, which is your destiny after fulfilling your purpose.

During this time, it is evident that we are in a battle to survive. People are leaving the church. People live in fear, wondering if they will survive another year, month, or day. They are concerned about their loved ones. The worldwide pandemic has taken its toll on finances, marriages, relationships, and health. God's commission to take the gospel to the world is more imperative today.

People are living and dying without the knowledge that Jesus saves. Some do not even know that there is a God. Some have not heard the message of salvation and may not accept Christ at your first attempt at sharing the gospel. However, you must plant the seed and allow God to water it and bring the person to conviction and acceptance of Jesus.

I wrote this book to encourage and strengthen you on your journey of fulfilling God's divine purpose for your life. If you confess and believe in Christ, you are His Ambassador! You must tell others and show them practical ways to accept Jesus as their Savior. People must hear of the greatest gift that God has to offer - salvation. It would be a sad commentary if there were no solution to the world's dilemma. Thank God there is an answer. I encourage you to tell people you come in contact with daily that "JESUS IS THE ANSWER!" He always was, and He always will be, the Way, the Truth, and the Life. There is no one greater. Take your journey, fulfilling God's divine purpose!

- Esther Luckett

TABLE OF CONTENTS

REFLECT ON THE PATH AND
JOURNEY GOD DESIRES US TO TAKE

Travel with me through this book for inspiration, encouragement, and strength along your journey, which begins on the Holy Highway. Do not forget to take a friend, neighbor, family member, colleague, or associate with you. If you have found the treasure of salvation, share the good news that Jesus saves. The Holy Highway will take you from earth to heaven. Tell somebody about this holy highway that leads to a place where the streets are made of gold, and the Lamb of God is the light. There is no pain, suffering, sickness, or crying there, but a place that Jesus went to prepare for all who accept Him as their Lord and Savior. God is looking to recruit soul winners who will win the lost and point them to Jesus. If each one of God's witnesses would win one person to Christ, the heavens will rejoice.

The Word of God says, "...I say to you that likewise there will be more joy in heaven over one sinner who repents than over ninety-nine just persons who need no repentance." Luke 15:7 Jesus said, "What man of you, having a hundred sheep, if he loses one of them, does not leave the ninety-nine in the wilderness, and go after the one which is lost until he finds it? And when he has found it, he lays it on his shoulders, rejoicing. And when he comes home, he calls together his friends and neighbors, saying to them, 'Rejoice with me, for I have found my sheep which was lost!" Luke 15:4-6

As you travel along your journey to fulfilling God-divine purpose, make sure to stop along the way to pray, praise, read your Bible, give thanks, count your blessings, and sing songs to encourage yourself in the Lord. In this book, there are "spiritual rest stops." Please take time to meditate and spend time reflecting on what you have read. It is essential to take time from your busy schedule and spend time with God.

CHAPTER 1

WHAT IS GOD'S PURPOSE AND PLAN FOR YOUR LIFE?

"God does not choose people because of their ability, but because of their availability." **Brother Andrew**

The Bible tells us, Jesus traveled through all the towns and villages of that time, teaching in the synagogues and announcing the good news about the Kingdom. He healed every kind of disease and illness. When he saw the crowds, he had compassion for them because they were confused and helpless, like sheep without a shepherd. He said to his disciples, "the harvest is plentiful, but the workers are few."

It is now your turn to pick up where our Savior and the disciples left off. Their journey has ended. The baton is passed on to you. Many people's souls depend on you to spread the news of the gospel before it is too late. Christ said if we are faithful, we will receive our reward. Besides the heavenly reward of the victory crown, you will have the recompense of knowing that you helped lead a dying soul to Christ. Just think, after fulfilling your purpose, "when your labor is over, and your work on earth is done, you will hear your Savior say, "well done, thou good and faithful servant."

In the work industry, some recruiters reach out to prospective employees via different mediums to find the best candidates for the positions they are looking to fill for various companies. The recruiter may request resumes for a position. If a person is a good fit, the recruiter may suggest the company hire the individual for the job. There are even some positions that are given because someone recommends you. It may be a father, mother, sister, brother, friend, associate, etc., who works for the company. They may tell you about the job and submit your name as a possible candidate. You go for an interview, and you are offered the position without having any experience. You are hired not because of your qualifications but because of who you know.

The Almighty God, our creator, the One who spoke and worlds came into being, is looking down searching among His creation for people who will respond to His call. God needs dedicated, willing workers, laborers who are eager to be part of His Kingdom building. The wonderful thing about this work is that anyone may qualify. All He asks is that you receive Him as your personal Savior, have a heart that is willing, be obedient, and be available. You may have nothing to offer right now, but there is no requirement. Someone once wrote, "Nothing in my hands I bring simply to the cross I cling." As you seek Him, the Lord will reveal your purpose to you. He left you with a fantastic guidebook written by people who took the journey before you. It is full of scriptures, instructions, directions, and the promises you need to be the best for Him.

God desires to use you in different ways and at different stages throughout your journey. No one is too young or too old. Your height, weight, looks, social status, and financial status do not matter when it comes to finding and fulfilling God's purpose for your life.

God needs all kinds of workers in His vineyard. He needs:

1. Ministers: Pastors, preachers, worship leaders, ministers of music, etc., who are willing to be used by God.

2. Christian educators, writers, and Sunday school teachers who are willing to teach God's word.

3. Intercessors and prayer warriors who are willing to work behind the scenes.

4. Technicians, cleaners, gardeners, etc., will help beautify the temple.

5. Missionaries and missionary helpers (local and international) to share the good news of the gospel.

6. Special workers to care for and visit the sick and shut-in the church and community using practical ways to share God's love (feeding the hungry, shopping for those who cannot leave the house, spending time with the elderly, etc.).

7. Caretakers of the Lord's money, honesty, and upright people of integrity monitoring and investing funds to help build up the kingdom of God.

He transformed my life and trained me to be His ambassador to spread the good news of the gospel. No one is truly worthy of God's grace, love, and mercy. He is God. The creator of the world and all that is in it. What a wonderful notion that God wants to use you and me. If you allow Him, he will give you the power you need to fulfill His commission. This is a journey you do not want to miss. Do not be afraid to accept the challenge. Pray, seek God, plan, and He will bring it to past. The benefits are out of this world.

"For we are His workmanship, created in Christ Jesus for good works, which God prepared beforehand that we should walk in them." Ephesians 2:10

NOTES: Write your thoughts and ideas of how this chapter has helped and inspired you on your spiritual journey.

_____

_____

_____

_____

_____

_____

_____

_____

_____

_____

_____

_____

_____

CHAPTER 2
DESTINED TO BE ALL THAT WANTS YOU TO BE

"Your call will become clear as your mind is transformed by the reading of Scripture and the internal work of God's Spirit. The Lord never hides His will from us. In time, as you obey the call first to follow, your destiny will unfold before you. The difficulty will lie in keeping other concerns from diverting your attention."
Swindoll Charles R.

_____

You are a child of God made in His image who has work to do with Kingdom building. Even if you are not a believer, if you are willing and accept Christ as your personal Savior, God can change your life and make you a person that He can use in incredible ways.

We live in a crucial time where the world is in dire need of God's love, joy, hope, compassion, and peace. People need to hear that Jesus loves them and gave His life to bring them salvation. Spreading the gospel is crucial because people have already died prematurely from the Coronavirus, social injustices, hurricanes, tornados, car accidents without the knowledge that Jesus died for them.

God needs people, filled with the indwelling Holy Spirit radiating through them, to light up the world. When your light is shining, people will be drawn to you and opens the door to sharing Jesus. God needs believers who will take their call seriously, be dependable, and are fully committed to the work of God. There are people in the world who are lost and living in darkness. The Lord needs the church to do the work necessary in this world to lead people out of darkness into the light of Christ.

"You are the light of the world. A city that is set on a hill cannot be hidden." Matthew 5:14

When Jesus spoke these words, He was talking to regular people who had gathered to hear Him speak. Jesus calls ordinary people to do extraordinary things. He chooses the impossible things in life and turns them into miracles. Suppose you accept His call to service. He will do amazing things through and with you.

The worldwide pandemic surprised us by bringing fear, anxiety, financial hardship, food insecurity, job loss, foreclosures, and risk of evictions, health challenges, and death. Many hospitals and nursing homes are full of patients who cannot see loved ones. People are dying from COVID-19 without the knowledge of who Christ is. Prisons are full of people who need to hear the gospel.

People are wondering when or if things will go back to normal. The signs of the times are everywhere. Although we are experiencing unprecedented times, God is still on the throne. The good news is that our omniscient God has strategically placed you in homes, jobs, neighborhoods, and other areas where you can do His work, be His hands, feet, and mouth, and heart to reach out, encourage and share the good news salvation. Wherever God has placed you can be your platform for sharing His love with those in need. The places you cannot go physically, you can travel on your knees.

The present pandemic did not take God by surprise. He was, is, and always will be the King of the World and omniscient (All-Knowing). He is actively at work in our lives. He is your present help in trouble; He is your comforter and defender. God's promise to you is He will never leave you nor forsake you. You can trust Him during this pandemic. He has everything under control. God wants you to work with him to get the Word out – "JESUS SAVES!" There is only one answer to the world's problems. "Jesus is the way, the truth, and the life," as recorded in the Word of God.

There are people around you who can benefit from the purpose God has ordained for you. Your gifts and talents can be used to reach out to a troubled soul. Today, men, women, and children are hungry and thirsty for something that will satisfy their bodies and souls. Jesus Is the answer! Sadly, the world turns to substitutes to fill their needs. Many turn to alcohol, drugs, promiscuous lifestyles, etc., a temporary fix.

They do not know Christ can fill that void in their life. If you do not tell them, how will they know? If you do not help them, how will their eyes be opened to the truth? Brothers, sisters, people of God, do not neglect your God-ordained purpose and miss the opportunity to help change a life for the better. It is the enemy's purpose to keep you from fulfilling your purpose of doing God's work. RISE, child of God, you are needed for this appointed time. The call may move you out of your comfort zone. You may have to change your position, location, etc., to reach a lost soul. Listen for God's voice giving you instructions on what He needs you to do. Stay tuned in to the Holy Spirit. At the right time, God will whisper what he needs you to do.

God may be calling you to do something that you do not understand. May your response be, "Lord, I am willing. You have His promises to be with you on your journey. He is more than able to help me fulfill my God-ordained destiny." Let God be glorified through you. It is the best decision you can ever make. He promises:

- **I will always be with you. – Joshua 1:9**
- **I will give you strength for the journey. – Isaiah 41:10.**
- **I will help you in the times of trouble. – Jeremiah 33:3.**
- **I will provide all your needs. – Philippians 4:19**
- **I will answer you when you call. – Jeremiah 33:3**
- **I will give you peace. – John 14:27**
- **I will always love you. – Jeremiah 31:3**
- **I will be your protector. – Psalm 34:7-8.**

Spend time in prayer with God. Take time to pray for yourself, your family, and others. Pray for added strength to get you through the next leg of your journey.

Prayer does not need a physical vehicle to get it to its destination. You can take your needs, petitions, and request to God on your knees in prayer. Prayer goes directly from your mouth to God's ears, and God dispatches the answer whenever and wherever it is needed.

I said, "Yes Lord, I'll take the job.
Your heart I want to please.
I'll heed Your call and swiftly go.
By traveling on my knees."
Written by Sandra Goodwin

NOTES: Write your thoughts and ideas of how this chapter has helped and inspired you on your spiritual journey.

CHAPTER 3
WORKING TOGETHER IN THE BODY OF CHRIST

"God is preparing His heroes. And when the opportunity comes, He can fit them into their places in a moment. And the world will wonder where they came from." **A. B. Simpson**

In God's church, there are many members with unique gifts and talents. The body of Christ consists of people of different genders, ethnicities, nationalities, cultures. There are different callings and elections that God has chosen specially for us. Although we are different and have different callings and jobs to do in the church, we must work together to fulfill the divine purpose of sharing the gospel to a lost world. Even in the church today, Christians are losing their faith, peace, joy, and hope. They too are struggling during this pandemic and time of social unrest. They have lost loved ones, jobs, and sources of income. They are wondering why these things are happening to them and are looking for a lifeline. We have that lifeline—the message of hope.

People need to know that Jesus loves them. When you are God's representative where people see Jesus by the way you live. If willing to share, you have the answer to all their fears. That is why Jesus commissioned us to carry the good news, "Go ye into all the world and preach the gospel." It was what the world needed over 2,000 years ago, and it is what the world needs now. We are obligated to be God's witnesses to people in person, as well as on social media (internet, zoom, Instagram, YouTube). It is vital to seek God in prayer and listen out for His instructions. All you have to do is ask, seek, and we shall find. God will reveal your divine purpose and the way you should share Him. If you are willing, you can be God's hands, feet, and mouth, and heart down here on earth.

Jesus tells us that how we treat others is how we treat God. We are all God's masterpiece, created in His image. We must be sensitive to people's needs. God hates sin, but He loves the sinner. When we are witnessing to people about Christ, we must remember we are not their judge.

When my children were young, they had an exceptional Bible study teacher, Sister Thelma. She taught them about the different 'Judges' in the Bible. She ended the lesson by telling the children that they are not judges and should take off the judge's robe when witnessing to classmates and peers. I took this lesson for myself when witnessing to people and telling them of the Savior. I always tell myself that I was once in their situation. My children were young when they were taught the lesson of not judging, which has impacted their lives. From that lesson, they learned to see all people as Jesus sees them. It is imperative to remember that God is the righteous Judge who shows mercy and grace.

We are all sinners, some saved by grace and others in need of God's mercy and grace. The Bible tells us, "We all have sinned and come short of the glory of God." Remember this: "he who turns a sinner from the error of his way will save a soul from death and cover a multitude of sins." James 5:20 God wants to use you to encourage people to seek the Lord. Let us bring people to Christ instead of causing them to reject Christ. This is our commission. To God, "All lives matter." It is not the Lord's will that any should perish. It does not matter what race, ethnicity, or culture, or gender a person is. Every individual is important to our Lord. Remember I discussed being God's hands, feet, mouth, and heart? Here is how:

GOD'S HANDS: Reach out to those in need in practical ways by providing food for the hungry. Give clothes, toiletries, a smile, a note, a letter of encouragement, or a card. Matthew 25:35-40

GOD'S FEET: Carry the gospel. Perhaps to your home, your job, your school, your community, or abroad. "And how can anyone preach unless they are sent? As it is written: How beautiful are the feet of those who bring good news! Isaiah 52:7 "and having shod your feet with the preparation of the gospel of peace." Ephesians 6:15

GOD'S MOUTH: Spread the saving grace of Christ to a world that is lost. After Jesus was crucified and resurrected, he left his followers with a message that has been passed down through time. The instructions are for you today: "Go therefore and make disciples of all the nations, baptizing them in the name of the Father and of the Son and of the Holy Spirit, teaching them to observe all things that I have commanded you; and lo, I am with you always, even to the end of the age." Amen. Matthew 28:19-20. We may not be able to physically speak to people face to face during this time of the pandemic, but God has orchestrated other ways to share His love and the good news of the gospel.

GOD'S HEART: Share the love of God with others. Look for opportunities to do good and to show kindness, compassion, forgiveness, etc. Show empathy to those who are hurting, especially during a difficult and challenging time. The blessings that God has poured out on you can be shared with others. Jesus is the perfect example of showing the love of the Father. He went around doing good to those who loved and despised Him. Jesus commands you to love as He loves. If we follow these principles when showing the love of God, we are sharing the heart of God with others.

"This is My commandment, that you love one another as I have loved you. Greater love has no one than this than to lay down one's life for his friends." John 15:12-13

"You have heard that it was said, 'You shall love your neighbor and hate your enemy. But I say to you, love your enemies, bless those who curse you, do good to those who hate you, and pray for those who spitefully use you and persecute you." Matthew 5:43-45

When you hear God's voice calling you, I pray that you respond to His call. The Apostle John gives us some sound advice when it relates to fulfilling God's divine purpose. He said, *"I must work the works of Him who sent Me while it is day; the night is coming when no one can work."* John 9:4

If God has strategically placed you where you interact with people (health care, hospitals, nursing homes, law enforcement, prisons, etc.), you have an excellent opportunity to be God's hands, feet, mouth, and heart.

Respond to God daily. Each day there are new ways to fulfill our calling and purpose. Take time to ponder and pray over each thought or instruction the Lord puts on your mind and heart. Agree with what the Lord needs you to do.

NOTES: Write your thoughts and ideas of how this chapter has helped and inspired you on your spiritual journey.

CHAPTER 4

"HERE AM I, LORD. SEND ME!"

Jesus followed the Heavenly Father's plan for His life.
His earthly purpose was to bring salvation to the world.
His name "Jesus" means "God Rescues." **E.A.L**

When God created humanity, He had a plan and purpose. God assigned Adam and Eve tasks to do in the beautiful Garden of Eden. Adam and Eve were given everything they needed to live a wonderful, productive life and a free will to choose between right and wrong. That same free will is yours today. When Adam and Eve decided to do things their way and disobey God's instructions, they were separated from God. Today, many continued to choose their way over God's, which caused them to be separated from God as well. Man's disobedience and sin grieved our loving Heavenly Father. Our Holy God could not look upon man because of sin. Something needed to be done to reconcile humanity back to God.

"Therefore, when He came into the world, He said: "Sacrifice and offering You did not desire, but a body You have prepared for Me. In burnt offerings and sacrifices for sin You had no pleasure. Then I said, 'Behold, I have come— In the volume of the book it is written of Me— To do Your will, O God.' " Hebrews 10:5-15

Who could bridge the gap between God and man? Who could appease God's anger and wash away the sin that separates man from God? Would one of the "Heroes of Faith" be worthy to undertake this great task? The heroes of the faith had passed off the scene. Could the Father send them back to earth? Who would be worthy of answering the call to save humanity?

These faithful men of God did great exploits but were not without sin.

Abraham: Was called to be the Father of many Nations.
Noah: Was called by God to build an ark to save people from a flood.
Joseph: Was sent to Egypt and called to save his family during a time of famine
Moses: Was chosen to deliver the people of Israel out of bondage.
Joshua: Was a successful leader who led his people into the Promised Land.
David: Was a man after God's own heart and went from shepherd boy to king.

None of these "heroes of faith" were worthy and able to answer the call to redeem a sinful man.

God was searching for someone who would accept the challenge. Who would be willing? Who would go? God chose Jesus, His only begotten son, who was there before the world was formed. He is a part of the trinity and Godhead. I can imagine the question being asked in Heaven, "Who will go? Whom can I send?" Jesus answering the call, "Here am I. Send Me." God's plan of salvation demanded a sacrifice. Jesus was the spotless Lamb of God who would take away the sin of the world.

"For God so loved the world that he gave his only begotten Son, that whosoever believeth in him should not perish, but have everlasting life." John 3:16

Jesus took His purpose seriously. He healed the sick, preached deliverance to those held captive by sin, gave sight to the blind, raised the dead, taught multitudes, and fed 5,000 thousand hungry people. Our Lord showed love to His neighbors and those who hated Him. He reached out to people who were outcasts in society. Jesus was the perfect example of who God wants you to pattern your life after. Our Lord and Savior, Jesus Christ, made a difference while he walked this earth. We, too, can make a difference, especially during this season of sickness, disease, and social unrest in the world.

On the cross, after completing His work and purpose of reconciling man back to God, Jesus cried out, "It is finished!" He fulfilled every promise God had given regarding His work on earth. His journey on earth was coming to an end. Jesus was about to begin another work as our High Priest and Advocate, making intercession to the Father on our behalf. When Christ went back to Heaven, He left the Holy Spirit to guide and support you as you begin the assignments He has commissioned you to do. *"And He said to them, "Go into all the world and preach the gospel to every creature."* Mark 16:15

Jesus paid it all, but we still have work to do. Will you allow God to fulfill His divine purpose through you? Will you answer the call? Remember, this is a journey, but you do not have to go alone. After Jesus commissioned His disciples, He left them with this promise: *"... and lo, I am with you always, even to the end of the age." Amen.* Matthew 28:20

Think of the Goodness of Jesus. Reflect on what The Lord has done for you thus far on your journey. "Praise the LORD! Oh, give thanks to the LORD, for He is good! For His mercy endures forever." Psalm 106:1

NOTES: Write your thoughts and ideas of how this chapter has helped and inspired you on your spiritual journey.

_____

_____

_____

_____

_____

_____

_____

_____

_____

_____

_____

_____

_____

_____

_____

_____

_____

_____

_____

_____

CHAPTER 5
BEING PREPARED TO FULFILL YOUR DIVINE PURPOSE

When I stand before God at the end of my life, I would hope that
I would not have a single bit of talent left, and could say,
'I used everything you gave me.'" **Erma Bombeck**

"What is that you have in your hands?"

Ambassadors of Christ, your purpose is to win souls for Christ. It
is not God's will that any should perish. It will be a terrible thing
to see people lose out on heaven because we did not take the
opportunity to share salvation when we had the chance. It is to
live for Christ and fulfill our commission while we have the
chance. Christ wants you to be faithful and obedient to God's
will. Like Jesus, God expects you to always be about your
Heavenly father's business. Have you ever wondered what God's
purpose is for you? I guess most Christians have thought about
this at one time or another. You may have asked yourself the
why, what, how, when, and where questions.

- Why am I here?
- What is God's purpose for my life?
- How can I be all that God wants me to be?
- When will I reach my divine purpose and destiny?
- Where will I be in 1, 5, 10, 15, 20 years, as it pertains to
  fulfilling my God-given purpose?

We are all designed to be a part of God's great master plan, and you have a role to play in kingdom building. Perhaps, you have realized your divine purpose and are already on your journey, busy working for your Lord and making a difference in this world that needs a Savior. Or, you might be in the seeking stage of the journey and are unsure of how to find your divine purpose. Do you want to be a worker in God's vineyard but need direction? Perhaps some of you have used your talents for self-gratification, but now we want to use them for God's glory and His kingdom.

Finding your talents, gifts, hobbies – Consider these methods below:

- What are things that I am good at doing? (i.e., art, music, speaking, writing, encouraging, singing, dancing, communicating, listening, reading, etc.).
- What are some things that I like to do?
- What are things that I like to purchase for leisure or luxury?
- What are things that I spend a lot of time working on when I have free time?
- What do people see me do and say, wow, you should do that full-time? Are you good at that? (refer to list above)
- Take notes of things you are good at and see how you can use them to bless and encourage others.
- Pray to God and ask Him to show you how He wants you to utilize the talents, gifts, and hobbies He has given you.

Moses, what is that you have in your hands?

Exodus 4:2-5 Miracles with the staff
Exodus 14:16 and 18-20 Parting of the Red Sea

A Rod: Moses had what he needed right in his hand to begin fulfilling the assignment that God had for him. God asked Moses, what is that you have in your hand? Moses had a staff in his hand. He left Egypt to go to Midian, where he was a shepherd for Jethro is called a priest. There he worked as a shepherd. God used Moses' staff to perform many miracles. Moses fulfilled His divine purpose of leading God's people out of bondage. As you follow Moses' journey, you will see how he gave God what he had, and God did through him and with him more abundantly above what Moses thought possible.
Let us looks at some things that God used in the Bible in the old and New Testament that seemed insignificant.

Let us looks at some things that God used in the Bible in the old and New Testament that seemed insignificant.

David, what is that you have in your hands?

I Samuel 17:26-50
A Sling and Five Smooth Stones: Young David had a sling, and five smooth stones picked up from a brook. When the enemies were threatening the people of God, the king, the soldiers were all afraid. David saw the opportunity to stand up and represent God in a situation that could have cost many people their lives. He felt God leading him to take on the challenge of defeating Goliath and saving God's people. Despite the negative comments from those who should have supported him, David allowed God to use what he had to fulfill his purpose of saving God's people. On his journey to fulfilling his destiny as the king of Israel, David used his music to soothe King Saul when he was angry and distressed. God used David to write many Psalms in the Bible, which have blessed the church and many Christians today.

Little boy, what is that you have in your hands?

John 6:1-14 and Matthew 14:13-21

Five Loaves and Two Fish: The child (lad) only had five loaves and two fish that his mother gave him for lunch. Jesus was teaching a large group of people (approximately 5,000). After teaching, Jesus told the disciples to sit the people down and feed them. The people had been listening to Jesus for a while with anything to eat. Our compassionate savior asked the disciples to give them something to eat. There was no food or store available to buy food. But there was a little boy with a lunch box in his hands. He offered it to the disciples to give to Jesus. The disciples said it was not enough to feed the crowd. Jesus said it was enough. Little boy, what is that in your hands? Give it to me. Jesus took the little boy's lunch, held it up to God, and He blessed it. He performed one of the greatest miracles passed down through history. The miracle of the feeding of five thousand was written in the Bible for your admonition and inspiration. In this passage, what is important to remember is that a little boy shared what he had. Age does not matter. God can use anyone willing to give their all to Him.

CHILD OF GOD, CREATED FOR HIS PURPOSE

What is that you have in your hands?

What do you have in your hands, in your possession? God knows, but do you know? He can take your talents, gifts, hobbies, dreams, aspirations, goals, brokenness, disabilities, etc., and use them for His glory! Seek Him and ask Him to reveal them to you.

Pray for added strength to get you through the next leg of your journey. Pray for the lost and their families. Pray for the leaders of the nations. Pray for whatever the Lord places on your heart during your quiet time.

NOTES: Write your thoughts and ideas of how this chapter has helped and inspired you on your spiritual journey.

_____

_____

_____

_____

_____

_____

_____

_____

_____

_____

_____

_____

_____

_____

_____

_____

_____

_____

_____

_____

CHAPTER 6

CHOOSING THE BETTER PART - SPENDING TIME WITH JESUS

"The world clamors, "Do more! Be all that you can be!"
But our Father whispers, "Be still and know that I am God."
Joanna Weaver

Does your life resemble Mary or Martha?

I love the story of Mary and Martha. There is so much to learn from the different experiences Martha and Mary had with Jesus. Martha reminds me so much of myself in some instances. I am always busy with something. My family calls me 'Busy Martha.' I rarely take time to "breathe." Every time there is a call for a volunteer, I put my name on the list. My friend used to tease me about having so much to do and so little time. "That was me." As I write this book, God shows me the changes I need to make as I travel on my journey. Jesus put it so well when he said to Martha, "Martha, Martha, you are worried and troubled about many things." Luke 10:41

Martha was busy doing necessary things but at the wrong time. She should have stopped serving when the "Word Made Flesh" was in her presence and began to teach. That was the time when she should have joined Mary sitting at the feet of Jesus. While Martha was busy trying to impress Jesus with her exceptional culinary and hostess skills, Mary gave her undivided attention. Jesus had something more significant that he wanted to share with Martha and Mary. But Martha didn't have the time.

There is always something calling for attention in our daily lives, but we must make time for Jesus. He has the answer to all that we need. He promises to give strength, peace, joy, and grace for the journey. If Martha had spent time with Jesus, she wouldn't have doubted Him when her brother Lazarus died. She became troubled and full of anxiety. She told Jesus, "If you had been here, my brother would not have died." Perhaps, during one of the times he was at her house, Jesus talked about being the resurrection and the life. Martha seemed to have missed it. Jesus reminded her of what was important. Mary chose to listen to Jesus' teaching - the better part. There is a time and a place for everything. You must select the better part that lasts for eternity. The food Martha prepared would last only for that day. But the living word Jesus shared with Mary stayed in her heart and comforted her when the Savior was crucified.

Mary was sat at Jesus' feet, learning, gaining the strength and knowledge needed to propel her into her destiny. God had work for Mary to do. She needed His guidance to be prepared for Him to use her in His service. Mary's previous lifestyle did not dictate who she was, for God had a better plan. She was destined for greatness. Mary Magdalene's divine calling and purpose was to anoint Jesus' body for His burial, evangelize and be witness to Christ's resurrection;

You, like Mary, have greatness to be displayed. Don't allow jealousy, busyness, past mistakes, or failures to hold you back from your God-ordained destiny. Those "hiccups," poor choices, poor judgments you make along the way to your future only serve to make you stronger, wiser, and more prepared for the work that God has for you. The journey will test your faith; your dedication, your diligence; your endurance. Do not let a Martha-type busyness cause you to neglect your responsibility. Spend time in prayer. Read His Word. Follow Mary's example of seeking wisdom, direction from the Master and learn what was planned before you were born. Jesus knows all the mistakes, challenges, and problems that will come to distract you from your God-given purpose divine destiny. Make God your priority.

"And Jesus' words to Martha are the words he wants to speak to your heart and mine:

"You are worried and upset about many things, but only one thing is needed."
The "one thing" is not found in doing more. It's found by sitting at his feet."
By: Joanna Weaver

Spend time with God. Ask what He wants you to do today. Listen out for His instructions. Agree with what the Lord needs you to do.

NOTES: Write your thoughts and ideas of how this chapter has helped and inspired you on your spiritual journey.

_____

_____

_____

_____

_____

_____

_____

_____

_____

_____

_____

_____

_____

_____

_____

_____

_____

CHAPTER 7
DO NOT BE AFRAID TO STEP OUT OF YOUR COMFORT ZONE

"Coming out of your comfort zone is tough in the beginning, chaotic in the middle, and awesome in the end...because in the end, it shows you a whole new world!! Make an attempt."
Manoj Arora

_____

God's purpose may call for you to leave your comfort zone. I am not talking about "God's comfort zone," where you are under God's divine protection or an area of safety where you are guided and comforted by the Holy Spirit (the comforter). You never want to leave "God's comfort zone." I am referring to "your comfort zone." It is a place where you feel most relaxed. You may not be happy, growing, or spiritually fruitful in your comfort zone. However, you think that you should stay there rather than meet with difficulties somewhere else. Perhaps you may be apprehensive of moving out of your comfort zone because you fear change. This is natural, but God wants you to let go of these feelings and let Him lead you. He promises to go with you. Sure, it may feel uncomfortable, most changes are. But if it is where God wants you to go and what He is calling you to do, He will work things out for you by going before you.

"For God has not given us a spirit of fear, but of power and of love and of a sound mind." 2 Timothy 1:7

Do not let what other people say stop you from fulfilling your purpose or accepting God's will for your life. Imagine Abraham's feelings when God called him to leave his family and homeland to fulfill his purpose. God told Abraham that his destiny was to be the father of many nations. Abraham had to leave his home (his comfort zone) and travel to an unfamiliar place where God sent him. His family and friends did not understand why he had to leave. They tried to convince him that it was a bad choice. Abraham did not live in a time like today, where he could pick up a cell phone and call for help if he found himself in trouble. He did not have Facetime, Zoom, Facebook, or other social media to connect with family and friends. He traveled a long distance to a place he had never been and knew nothing about. There were no airplanes, cars, or trains to get him there comfortably. Abraham could not make reservations for lodging. There was no job lined up when he got to where God was sending him. I am sure that Abraham was uncomfortable leaving all he knew behind and venturing into the unknown. Despite the odds against him, Abraham embarked on his journey to fulfilling God's purpose for His life.

Do not let fear keep you from obeying God's will. You may not know what tomorrow holds or where God will lead you. It may call for you to leave your comfort zone—the place where you feel most at home, secure, and at ease. Moses' comfort zone was Midian. He fled Egypt and ran to Midian, where he hid for 40 years. However, God did not forget him. God still had work for Moses to do. God was training Moses to be a leader of His people. When Moses finally accepted the call on his life to lead Israel's children out of bondage, he asked God, whom should I tell Pharaoh sent me?

God said to Moses, "Tell him I AM sent you." God was speaking to Moses, as He says to you today: I AM with you; I AM your refuge and strength; I AM a present help in the time of trouble; I AM the lover of your soul. He promises that He will never leave and be with you on your journey, leading, guiding, and protecting you as you fulfill His purpose. Nothing takes God by surprise. He has everything under control. Always remember, your Heavenly Father knows what your tomorrow holds. Do not be afraid to take that next step. He asks you to leave your comfort zone so that you can be a comfort to others.

Your Spiritual Rest Stop

Stop and count your blessings—God's blessings on you, your family, and your friends. Stop and encourage yourself in the Lord.

"David was greatly distressed because the men were talking of stoning him; each one was bitter in spirit because of his sons and daughters. But David found strength in the Lord his God." 1 Samuel 30:6 (NIV)

NOTES: Write your thoughts and ideas of how this chapter has helped and inspired you on your spiritual journey.

_____

_____

_____

_____

_____

_____

_____

_____

_____

_____

_____

_____

CHAPTER 8
ARE YOU DOING YOUR BEST FOR JESUS?

"Faithful servants never retire. You can retire from your career,
But you will never retire from serving God."
Rick Warren

_____

As we come to the end of this book, I cannot stress enough how important it is to answer the call and remain faithful to your calling and commission. The sovereign Lord has placed many in your life who are depending on you in the form of immediate and extended family; spouse, brothers and sisters, unbelieving friends, co-workers, neighbors' classmates, and associates. The gospel these people will hear or see lived may only come from you. God has given you gifts, talents, resources, knowledge, and finances that can be useful in helping the lost find the Savior. There will be people along your journey watching to see if you are faithful to our calling. The way you live your life can influence others to seek the Lord. Your life is a book that is read and studied by many. Your testimony will impact those you come in contact with daily and can determine if contact will have a positive or negative effect. The choice is yours.

All that Jesus asks of you is that you live a life that is pleasing to Him. Ask yourself, "If God calls me home tomorrow, have I made someone else's life better? Have I done my best for Jesus?" You don't want to have any guilt or regrets because you neglected to help someone or tell someone about Jesus. That beggar on the street that you walked by and looked the other way, that family next door who was hungry and struggling because a spouse lost their job, a grieving co-worker of a friend you could have taken time to console. When your life work is ended, and your work on earth is completed, live so that you will hear your Heavenly Father say, "well done, thou good and faithful servant."

Take time for another rest stop and meditate on as you travel on your journey is, "Have I done my best for Jesus?" When it is all said and done, this is what will count the most.

Jesus is coming back again to take His loved ones home to heaven. That is why it is so essential that you fulfill your God-given purpose and calling. I pray that as you have taken the journey through this book, you are inspired, encouraged, and motivated to fulfill your calling and commission. Tell someone today about the Savior who gave His life to bring them salvation. Jesus is commissioning and re-commissioning His workers. Will you respond to His call today?

We mustn't listen to negative voices telling us it is impossible to fulfill God's purpose for our lives. Remember, God IS the God of the God of the IMPOSSIBLE. Listen to His voice speaking to your heart, revealing your purpose. The world needs Jesus, and Jesus needs you. Do not be too busy to hear God's voice when He calls you. He has strategically placed you where you are today. All He wants is you. DON'T MISS YOUR OPPORTUNITY. Martha was too busy. Judas was too greedy; Thomas doubted, and Jonah said No! If you respond to the call, "Here I am, Lord, use me." And you are faithful until the end. There is a crown awaiting you.

"Therefore, my beloved brethren, be steadfast, immovable, always abounding in the work of the Lord, knowing that your labor is not in vain in the Lord." 1 Corinthians 15:58

Your Spiritual
Rest Stop

It's prayer and reflection time. Spend more time with God, it will give you strength for the next leg of your journey.

"Then he said to his disciples, "The harvest is plentiful, but the laborers are few; therefore pray earnestly to the Lord of the harvest to send out laborers into his harvest." Matthew 9:37-38

NOTES: Write your thoughts and ideas of how this chapter has helped and inspired you on your spiritual journey.

_____

_____

_____

_____

_____

_____

_____

_____

_____

_____

_____

_____

_____

_____

ADDITIONAL NOTES AND THOUGHTS

"Cast your cares on him for He cares for you." – 1 Peter 5:7

_____

_____

_____

_____

_____

_____

_____

_____

_____

_____

_____

_____

_____

_____

_____

_____

_____

_____

ADDITIONAL NOTES AND THOUGHTS

ADDITIONAL NOTES
AND THOUGHTS

ADDITIONAL NOTES
AND THOUGHTS

_____

_____

_____

_____

_____

_____

_____

_____

_____

_____

_____

_____

_____

_____

_____

_____

_____

_____

_____

_____

_____

_____

_____

ADDITIONAL NOTES AND THOUGHTS

ADDITIONAL NOTES AND THOUGHTS

REFERENCES

Preface:
"Sometimes it takes a mountain" by Mark Mathes and Gloria Gaither
"Take the wheel," by Carrie Underwood.

All scripture is from the NKJV version of the Bible.

1 Corinthians 15:58
2 Chronicles 7:14
1 Peter 5:7
2 Timothy 1:7
Ephesians 2:10
Ephesians 6:15
Exodus 14:16 & 18-20
Exodus 4:2-5
Hebrews 10:19-20
Hebrews 10:5
I Samuel 17:26-50
Isaiah 41:10
Isaiah 52:7
James 5:20
Jeremiah 31:3
Jeremiah 33:3
Jeremiah 33:3
John 14:1-4
John 14:27
John 15:12-13
John 3:16

John 9:4.
Joshua 1:9
Luke 10:41
Luke 15:4-6
Luke 15:7
Mark 16:15
Matthew 14:13-21
Matthew 16:24
Matthew 25:35-36
Matthew 25:35-40
Matthew 25:40
Matthew 28:19-20
Matthew 28:20
Matthew 5:14
Matthew 5:43-45
Matthew 9:37-38
Philippians 4:19
Psalm 106:1
Psalm 34:7 - 8
St. John 6:1-14

Esther Albert-Luckett resides in White Plains, NY, with her husband, two children, and her 93-year old mother. She is a minister, educator, and Sunday school teacher. Esther is also the Assistant for "Kids Presents," a program that provides children the opportunity to take what they have learned through arts or STEM and share their knowledge with their community. She has always been highly active as a writer, educator, and event planner for her church's programs and events.

She has over 30 years in the banking industry. Being led by God, Esther is pursuing a master's degree in Early Childhood Education/Behavioral Science. She follows God's leadings as she continues on her journey in fulfilling God's divine purpose for her life. Her motto is, "Don't give up your dreams and aspirations, for, with God, all things are possible if you believe.

CPSIA information can be obtained
at www.ICGtesting.com
Printed in the USA
BVHW091119130921
616657BV00019B/507